ART NOUVEAU

Peter Bramböck

TIGER BOOKS INTERNATIONAL
LONDON

© 1988 by I.P. Verlagsgesellschaft
International Publishing GmbH, München
Published in 1988 for
Tiger Books International Limited, London
ISBN 1-870461-60-6
Printed and bound by Brepols N.V.-Turnhout, Belgium
Translation: Donal McLaughlin

Acknowledgement
The author and publishers wish to thank Messrs Holle,
Baden-Baden, for the use of pictures and copyright.
As far as the works of the artists Aman, Bakst, Behrens,
Denis, Heine, Hohlwein, Matisse, Mucha and Vogeler are
concerned the copyright in held by VG Bild-Kunst, Bonn,
SPADEM, Paris, Beeldrecht, Amsterdam, 1988; for the artists
Kandinsky and Kokoschka the copyright is hold by
COSMOPRESS, Geneva, 1988.

In quest of a new style

No epoch in European Art has ever undergone such a radical, rapid, and far-reaching change as that which marks the years around 1900. Within a period of twenty to thirty years, the transition from Classicism to Modern Art took effect at that time; this development was symbolized by the step into a new century. The quest for a new style was not only inspired, however, by the impatient urge to move forward, such as is the privilege of every young generation; it resulted in the first instance from a rejection of the old, which had been marked by the academic traditions governing the schools of art throughout the nineteenth century. The new generation wanted nothing more to do with courtly rococo, the Biedermeier style of the bourgeois, a classicism rooted in antiquity, and historical paintings which glorified the deeds of national heroes, past and present. A further important contribution was made to this development by the Industrial Revolution which peaked in the nineteenth century. The French Revolution of 1789 had introduced the democratization of society; the Industrial Revolution in the century which followed, on the other hand, epitomized economic and technological progress, but it robbed mankind of some part of its newly acquired freedom by subjecting it to new constraints, namely those imposed by machines, the symbol of mass production, but also of mass consumption. The first international industrial exhibition, the Great Exhibition in London in 1851, united the countries of the world in the form of a technological self-portrait, but it led, too, to a rejection of the crude materialism on display there. So it is not surprising that the renewal of applied arts begins in Great Britain. This development was to become an essential part of Art Nouveau.

At this point in our historical survey, we must now introduce the concept of "the synthesis of the arts", an idea which arose in Britain, and found its perfection in Germany and Austria. The quest there for a new style did not only relate to art; it was also a quest for a new lifestyle, for individuality. All those things which surround man in his daily life were to be fashioned artistically, and so be distinguishable from those objects massproduced by industry. Architecture, furniture, glassware, jewellery, carpets, wallpaper – all these things were re-designed with the aim of awakening in man an altered, a positive, a vital consciousness. What was

understood by "art" was expanded simultaneously to include commercial crafts, and so, around the turn of the century, e.g. in Munich, workshops dealing in arts and crafts united to form an association which still exists today ("Vereinigte Werkstätten für Kunst im Handwerk"); in Austria, the Viennese Workshop ("Wiener Werkstätte") was created. Their products were reserved for the well-to-do in society, but the idea of "the synthesis of the arts" later led, for example, to the founding of the Bauhaus school, which aimed to design everyday, practical objects which functioned as perfectly as possible, were as beautiful as possible in terms of artistic creation, and which nevertheless could be produced by industry; these people thus pioneered what is known today as industrial design.

The population at large shared in Art Nouveau in another area of life, however, as early as the turn of the century; we have thus arrived at the actual theme of the present book: the graphic arts and the art of printing created by representatives of Art Nouveau. New printing processes invented in the second half of the nineteenth century made possible the reproduction of polychromatic submissions, with the number of copies published being practically unrestricted; the representatives of Art Nouveau availed themselves of this possibility. "The synthesis of the arts" in daily life was to find expression in books and periodicals too; their illustrations would please the eye of the reader, stimulate his imagination, and once again give rise to a new and vital consciousness. Educational and political intentions often formed the basis of such endeavours: art was to become popular, and common property; the population was to take pleasure in it, but the public's taste in art was to be educated and cultivated too. In every European country, numerous periodicals were founded at that time: in Paris, the "Revue Blanche" (1891); in London, "The Studio" 1893); in Berlin, "Pan" (1895); in Munich, "Simplicissimus" and "Jugend" (both 1896); and in Vienna, "Ver Sacrum" (1898), – to name just the most important fora for the new art, which was not necessarily identical with Art Nouveau.

In protest against the traditional view of art, numerous new groups of artists were founded at that time too. These broke away from the academic centres of art, as is expressed by the key term "Secession"; in ancient

Rome the "secessio plebis" occurred, the withdrawal of the people, who left the town in protest, with the intention of establishing on nearby hills a new Rome which was to realize better the desires and goals of the citizens. This antique form of protest against the traditional and ancient is mirrored in the foundation of "Secessions" in Munich (1892), in Vienna (1897), and in Berlin (1898).

Despite sharing the same name the painters and graphic artists who came together in these groupings by no means followed a common artistic path. Nor did there exist in Europe a more or less uniform and coherent Art Nouveau. The label "Jugendstil" exists only in Germany, but it would be wrong to suppose that it is taken from the title of the periodical "Jugend" – its origins are unclear. In Britain, for example, the (at that time) new direction in art was called "Modern Style"; in Italy "Stile floreale" or "Stile Liberty"; in Holland "Nieuwe Kunst"; and in France "Art Nouveau". And so we come to a division in the new style of French painting which, despite all the mutual influences, set off on tracks different from those followed by the new artistic course in most other European countries. In France at that time the points were shifted for the development of Modern Art. Between 1860 and 1870, Impressionism had come to the fore there, a direction in painting which was the result of the artist sensing nature, of the subjective perception of nature; this movement can thus also be regarded as a reaction against the process of mechanization which spread so very far in the nineteenth century. The subjective and artistic perception of nature, characteristic for the paintings of the Impressionists, no longer satisfied the new generation of artists; they wished to fathom the essence of things, and no longer illustrate them in a less or more naturalistic manner. A mode of depiction determined purely by notions of aesthetics was soon to give way to an artistic translation which rendered the essential. For this reason, artists worked only in their studios, and from their memory of impressions gained in, and from, nature. The logical results of this development were Symbolism, Expressionism and Abstract Painting, all of which were to have such an impact on twentieth-century art.

The illustrations

Josef Maria Auchentaller (1865–1949)
13   A Winters's Tale
Pen and ink, colour, 1901, 18.6 x 18.1 cm. Illustration for the month of February in the "Ver Sacrum" calendar of 1901.
Josef Maria Auchentaller, largely forgotten nowadays, was one of the founding members of the Viennese "Secession" to which he belonged until 1905. The reason for this lack of fame is that after his studies in Vienna and his professorship in Munich (1893–95), he moved to Grado in the Adria as early as 1901, where he became Commander of the Fishing Fleet in the local harbour, and where he died in 1949. His main period of artistic production lies between the years 1898–1909. During this time he created numerous posters, above all, however, pen-and-ink drawings and lithographs for the periodical "Ver Sacrum", the organ of the Viennese "Secession". Our illustration shows a "Winter's Tale": three masked girls in ball gowns, just the thing for the Carnival month of February, in an ornamental frame which is matched by the gold trimmings of the dresses. In the movements of the three girls, allusions to the snake-dance can be recognized which in those years was made popular in Europe by the American dancer Loie Fuller, and which inspired imaginative and mysterious works of art by many contemporary artists.

Aubrey V. Beardsley (1872–1898)
14   Book illustration for "Le Morte d'Arthur" by Thomas Malory
Autotype, 1983/94, approx. 18.2 x 12.7 cm.
15   Book illustration for "Salomé" by Oscar Wilde
Autotype, 1894, 17.8 x 12.6 cm.
No other representative of the Art Nouveau has made such a lasting impact as Aubrey V. Beardsley. Dozens of book illustrators, especially in Germany, have looked to his work for directions; advertising graphics, especially in the early twentieth century, but in the present too, have built on his achievement, and ten or twenty years ago every youth decorated his room with at least one Beardsley poster! This incredible (long-term) success is all the more remarkable when you consider that Beardsley died at the age of twenty-six and was active artistically for only six of those years. He was, moreover, self-taught. The insurance agent drew until 1892 only in his spare time and for his own personal enjoyment, following classical models such as Dürer, Michelangelo, and Botticelli. Then he became acquainted with Edward Burne-Jones (see 18, 19) and William Morris, but above all with the publisher J.M. Dent, who was looking for someone to illustrate Thomas Malory's "Morte d'Arthur", the legends of King Arthur and his Round Table; these tales, first published in 1485, reflected the fears of the times which now seem macabre, and lamented the world in a manner which clearly touched a nerve 400 years later in a new and (on the surface) quite different age. Beardsley delivered sample drawings which satisfied the publisher, and Dent commissioned the illustrations. What was required of Beardsley was just about impossible: in a few months he had to produce twenty large illustrations (one of which is Illustration 14 in this volume), as well as more than 500 borders, ornaments, vignettes and edgings. This enormous challenge caused Beardsley to find his own style within an extremely short period of time: an abstraction of nature, stylized and far removed from reality, modelled on medieval wood-engravings and Japanese models. His work can seem stilted and artificial to many a spectator, but it exerts an (inexplicable) fascination which one cannot escape.
The morbid nature of his era is mirrored too in Beardsley's illustration for Oscar Wilde's "Salomé" (15). In this work, the theme of sexuality shifts into the foreground, a

theme which conceals both promise and death, a yearning for the forbidden, and punishment for over-stepping bourgeois conventions – typical for the fin-de-siècle! Beardsley's depiction is completely in keeping with this: the spectator succumbs to the spirited veil-dance of Salome, just like King Herod who was prepared to pay what she demanded for it (New Testament, Matthew 14,7). And the price for the dance is high: in the Bible, it is the head of John the Baptist; today, it is surely the head of man in general! The strict use of line, inspired by Japanese models, and the two-dimensionality of the illustration convey an illusion of security, which is cancelled by a certain lasciviousness hinting at the depths of human sexuality, a chaos of feelings and longings which each of us senses in ourselves at some point, over which one can triumph, or before which one can fall.

William H. Bradley (1868–1962)
16   The Chap Book
Cover illustration, 1895
The World Exhibition in Chicago in 1893 proved to its European visitors that Art Nouveau had caught on in America too. Its most outstanding representative was William H. Bradley, a printer by trade, who had been working since the beginning of the 1890s as a draughtsman, illustrator and poster-artist. His works soon caused controversy as they followed in the immediate footsteps of Beardsley (see 14, 15). They concentrated more, however, on the decorative element than on the pictorial statement, but arrived in this way at an independent and artistic form. From 1894 onwards, the periodical "The Chap Book" appeared, for which Bradley produced numerous title pages (see illustration). The periodical reflected the newest developments in the fields of literature and graphic art; English and French, as well as American, artists contributed. From the beginning of the twentieth century onwards, Beardsley devoted himself in the main to typography, and, in the course of more than fifty years of activity, became America's leading artist in the field of printing.

Hugo L. Braune (born 1872)
17   Illustration for a heroic saga
Autotype, 1900, approx. 36 x 28 cm.
Of Hugo L. Braune we only know that after studying at the art school in Weimar, he lived in Berlin and was active as a war painter during World War I. The illustration of a heroic saga included here comes from a portfolio of the periodical "Insel", which appeared in four instalments between December 1899 and November 1900. Each instalment contained six original works by living artists, and four reproductions of works by older Masters. The periodical itself, conceived as a literary equivalent of the magazine "Pan", appeared from October 1899 onwards; famous artists of the time contributed. The periodical, like the publishing company "Insel" which later grew out of it, was an important podium for the artistic books of the German "Jugendstil" (see 42). Braune's illustration is included here as an example of an artistically successful piece of Art Nouveau which, however, in its mythologization of Teutonicism, has already taken the first step on a path which ended in the aberrations of National Socialism.

Edward Burne-Jones (1833–1898)
18   The Well at the World's End
Wood-engraving, 1896, 27.8 x 19 cm
19   The Golden Legend (Legenda aurea)
Wood-engraving, 1892, 24 x 17.5 cm
Both these illustrations confront us with several things which were decisive for the development of Art Nouveau in Britain: with the Pre-Raphaelites who pioneered the wholly artistic production of books; William Morris;

and his friend of many decades, Edward Burne-Jones. But let us take things in the correct order! At the beginning of the nineteenth century, a group of artists who called themselves the Nazarenes was formed in Rome; German Romanticism was their point of departure. They modelled themselves on late-medieval painting, especially on Italian painting before Raphael, and demanded true, immediate sensation in artistic creation. In this way they placed themselves in opposition to academic painting, and brought a new, sentimental, anti-classical trait into artistic creation, which was to be of paramount importance for the whole of the century, and which peaked in Art Nouveau. British painters imported these ideas to the island around the middle of the century, where the Brotherhood of the Pre-Raphaelites was quickly formed, with Dante Gabriel Rossetti (1828–1882) as its leading representative. This group also modelled itself on Italian painting before Raphael (hence the name of the group); its art, however, is characterized by a (frequently crude) juxtaposition of strong symbolism and sometimes banal realism, and, on the whole, by a sentimentality quite in keeping with the underlying atmosphere of fin-de-siècle. This was the great hey-day of industry (especially in Britain), which meant many advantages for man, but which also placed restrictions on his senses, and limited the imaginativeness of his thinking. The artists recognized this and fled into a medieval dream-world which conjured up before them the fulfilment of their desires.
Edward Burne-Jones studied theology and moved to Exeter College in Oxford in 1853, where he became acquainted with William Morris, with whom he was to share a life-long friendship. A year later, at art exhibitions, he was confronted with the works of the Pre-Raphaelites, and he decided, like Morris, to become a painter. On trips to France and Italy both studied the Gothic style. Morris soon tended towards arts and crafts which he saw as an alternative to mass-production in industry. With this in mind, he founded a firm in 1861, and Burne-Jones, among others, became a partner, although he remained above all a watercolour painter until 1870. Thereafter he became more and more enthusiastic about the ideas of William Morris, who, in his workshops, set him the task of delivering designs for carpets, mosaics, glass windows etc., in which the strict form and treatment of line in the Gothic style were the determining factors. In this way, Burne-Jones took the step from the Pre-Raphaelites to Art Nouveau, from the symbolic to the decorative. Above all, this development found expression in his work on artistic books. In 1891, Morris founded the Kelmscott Press in London; Burne-Jones and other significant artists worked together on this project, and produced a large number of beautifully crafted books, perfect examples of book ornamentation. Our illustrations (18, 19) come from books by this publishing company. The influence of the Pre-Raphaelites is very clearly recognizable in Illustration 19, an illustration for the "Legenda aurea", a thirteenth-century description of the lives of the saints, for the angel-figures could be by Rossetti. Very typical too is the framing of the illustrations with a linear ornamental edge, which borrows its forms from the Gothic style, as well as from cultic and Germanic jewellery. British art books of that period were for decades to determine the direction taken in that craft in Europe, and especially by the representatives of Art Nouveau in Munich and Vienna.

Harry Clarke (1890–1931)
20   Illustration for Edgar Allan Poe
Autotype, no date, approx. actual size
This illustration for Poe's "Tales of the Grotesque" must have been produced between 1910 and 1920, and

shows very nicely how long and to what a decisive degree the elements of Art Nouveau introduced by Beardsley continued to influence book illustration in Britain. Clarke, born and buried in Dublin, also illustrated Pope's "Rape of the Lock", Hans Christian Andersen's fairy-tales, and Goethe's "Faust". He acquired early fame between 1911 and 1913 with his designs for glass windows which were awarded gold medals.

Walter Crane (1845–1915)

21   Illustration for A Floral Fantasy in an Old English Garden
Autotype, 1899, 19.9 x 14 cm

Floral symbolism played an important role in European Art Nouveau. In the late Middle Ages artists had been acquainted with such symbols, they had subsequently been forgotten, and then rediscovered by the Romantics ("The Blue Flower"). The adjective "floral" is readily associated with Art Nouveau, for flowers, plants, blossoms, and leaves feature repeatedly as an essential decorative, but also as a symbolic element in works from around the turn of the century. The flower as a symbol of fertility, of the feminine, of sexuality, is often portrayed in detail, in a manner which highlights similarities with male and female genitals. In our illustration the group of women wear calyxes as head-dresses, indeed, for protection even, since the accompanying text indicates that the pretty young maids, with careless hearts and quite unheeding, disregard the young man in the foreground, from whose resting-place rise the phallus-like blossoms of several Aaron's rods.

Walter Crane, with his numerous publications, was the main theorist of Art Nouveau in Britain. His father was a miniature painter, and certain echoes of that genre can be found in our illustration. As an academic teacher, Walter Crane was mentor to a whole generation of artists who subscribed to the new style; he thus represents the link in the chain between the Pre-Raphaelites and Art Nouveau. Just like Morris and Burne-Jones (see 18, 19), with whom he worked together, he demanded a unity of text and illustration in book ornamentation; he formulates this idea in his book, "Line and Form". Between 1869 and 1875 he illustrated numerous volumes of fairy-tales which realized this unity. Way ahead of all his contemporaries, he anticipated in his use of line what was to become, ten years later, the highlight of graphic art in European Art Nouveau.

Josef Hoffmann (1870–1956)

22   Two Designs for House Entrances
Pen and ink, 1898, actual size, from "Ver Sacrum", Vol. 1, No. 7, p. 14.

The founding member of the Viennese "Secession", the architect and graphic artist Josef Hoffmann, is one of those representatives of Art Nouveau who realize most consistently the notion of "the synthesis of the arts" in their work. Dozens of public and private buildings were erected according to his plans (mainly in Vienna, but the famous Palais Stoclet in Brussels should be mentioned above all); he designed furniture, wallpaper, crockery, and jewellery. From 1899 onwards he was Professor of Architecture at the College of Commercial Art in Vienna; in 1903 he co-founded the Viennese Workshop, of which he was a member until its financial ruin in 1932; in 1912 he founded and then led the Austrian arts and crafts society. Even between 1949 and 1952, when he was well advanced in years, municipal housing schemes in Vienna were planned by him. The two designs for house entrances illustrated here were never realized. They reveal an unrealistic wealth of curves, typical for the style of the Viennese "Secession" at that time, but from which Hoffmann was soon to distance himself more and more; he found his way rapidly towards strict and regular recurring patterns which led to polished, standardized stylistic elements. His items of furniture could now be constructed in series, and could be arranged as people wished in apartments without the unity of the overall impression being lost. In the sphere of architecture, the equivalent intention was realized in the form of housing schemes, to which Hoffmann turned more and more. In 1907 the

young Le Corbusier met up with him; Le Corbusier's pilgrim church in Ronchamp, built between 1950 and 1954 on the foothills of the Vosges mountains, is vaguely reminiscent, in terms of the plasticity of its construction, of the architectural sketches by Josef Hoffmann included in this book.

Fritz Endell (1873–1955)

23   The Wave
Colour wood-engraving on Japanese paper, approx. 1900/1902, 26 x 11.7 cm

After studying theology, Fritz Endell turned to painting, influenced by his brother August, a self-taught interior designer, who at the end of the 1890s had written about an art "which rouses man's soul simply by means of shapes which resemble nothing familiar, which depict nothing and symbolize nothing, (an art) which relies on freely invented forms for its effect, just as music does on freely selected notes". These words can be applied to the colour wood-engraving "The Wave" by his brother Fritz, even if we are perhaps reminded of Homer's Aphrodite who sprang from the foam of the sea. From the sea grows a mermaid, the concrete combines with the fantastic, ornament becomes life. However attractive this wood-engraving seems, one cannot help feeling that Endell has taken Art Nouveau to a point here which permits of no further development; it collapses inwardly, just like a wave consumed by its own energy.

Wassily Kandinsky (1866–1944)

24   Wood-engravings from the portfolio "Xylographies"
1907, all 14.2 x 14.4 cm

No other artist of the Modern Era underwent such a gross and sudden change in his approach as Wassily Kandinsky and yet had such an enduring influence on his contemporaries. After studying Law and Economics in Moscow, the city of his birth, he at first became an outside lecturer, but ceased his academic activity in 1897 to devote himself to painting. That same year he went to Munich and soon afterwards became a student of Franz von Stuck (see 30, 57). With the sole interruptions of trips to Paris, Northern Africa, and Italy, he lived in Munich until 1914, had then to emigrate to Switzerland, and was appointed Professor at the Art Academy in Moscow in 1918. In 1921 he returned to Germany and, until 1933, was Professor at the "Bauhaus" in Weimar and Dessau; when the National Socialists seized power, he emigrated to Paris where he died eleven years later. His early works, influenced by his teacher Stuck, reveal a closeness to Art Nouveau. As both our illustrations show, Russian folklore has left its stamp on them; similar motifs can be found too in the work of Chagall, twenty years Kandinsky's junior. Both illustrations come from a collection of wood-engravings which appeared in 1907. Three years later Kandinsky painted his first abstract painting; in 1911 he was a founding member of the "Blauer Reiter" (Blue Rider), a group of artists in Munich, to which Macke, Marc, Klee, and Jawlensky belonged. A revolution had taken place in art, namely a movement towards abstract, non-representational art. And that was the most logical development of a set of problems which many representatives of Art Nouveau tried to master: freeing oneself from the object; trying to fathom the essentiality hidden behind the outward forms of nature.

Jessie Marion King (1876–1949)

25   Illustration for "The Magic Grammar"
Autotype, 1902, approx. 23.5 x 17 cm

If one considers how often in Art Nouveau the woman, female eroticism, is examined, and how often the woman is elevated as the giver of life, a symbol of fertility, it is astonishing that there is hardly a single female representative of this artistic style. On the other hand, this fact is perhaps an expression of the changing social role of women around the turn of the century, to which men reacted in an uncertain manner. The woman as mother, as a concubine, as a vamp, as the object of sexual desire, or as a danger to a male principle which manifested itself, at the end of the 19th century, above

all in a faith in technology? We are much more likely to find answers to these questions in Viennese Art Nouveau, which was confronted with the results of research by Sigmund Freud, than in the graphic prints by Jessie Marion King. She studied at the Glasgow School of Art, and was later Head of the Department of Book-binding there. As someone with an affinity to applied art, she produced designs for wallpaper and silk curtains, and her lightness of touch can be sensed in the illustration reproduced here, which was first printed in the forum of British Art Nouveau, the periodical "The Studio". The influence of Burne-Jones (see 18, 19) and Beardsley (14, 15) is unmistakable.

Aristide Maillol (1861–1944)

26   The Wave
Wood-engraving, from around 1898, 17 x 19.5 cm

The French sculptor, graphic artist and painter is mainly known to us for his plastic art, to which he turned his attention in the 1880s, or for his book illustrations which were printed between 1925 and 1938. The latter, although they were produced much later, reveal, in their logically consistent use of line, a link with his graphic art, executed in the Art Nouveau style, of which our illustration is an example. The presentation is completely different, however, from that which we experienced in the treatment of the same theme by Fritz Endell (23). Maillol's penchant for sculpture can be seen in the plasticity of the girl's body, round which swirling water laps; despite the restive lines which clearly suggest the strength of the wave and the dangers it poses, the girl's body rests peacefully there; only her right hand playfully resists the disturbance caused by the waves.

Henri Matisse (1869–1954)

27   Female Nude
Linocut, approx. 1906–1910, 47.3 x 38.5 cm

We already discovered a hint of Expressionism in the work of Maillol (26); it can be discerned even more clearly in this linocut by Henri Matisse. What, in Maillol's case, still seems rounded-off and static, is in a state of dissolution in the work of Matisse; his female nude seems truly to be threatened by the waves – their inclusion creates a dissonance, even if the woman's hair, portrayed in the same characteristic style as the waves, appears to point to a harmony with the element of water. One is almost tempted to switch round the titles of the two illustrations: Matisse's depiction seems to come closer to the theme of "The Wave" than does Maillol's static wood-engraving, for which "Female Nude" would be a more appropriate title. On the other hand, his girl responds actively to the element of water, whereas Matisse simply confronts the woman asleep in the deck-chair with the water.

Henri Matisse began by studying Law, was a student of the Parisian Académie Julian from 1890, and subsequently of the Ecole des Beaux Arts. Initially he had an affinity to Impressionism, but he turned away from this around 1900, influenced by Cézanne, and then found his way towards the expressionist style typical of him which made him the outstanding leader of the new force in France, the "Fauves", literally "the wild beasts".

Edward Okun (1872–1945)

28   Cover for the periodical "Chimera"
Pen and ink, 1902, 22 x 18 cm

Edward Okun is a Polish representative of Art Nouveau whom we would like to introduce. Okun studied in Warsaw, Cracow, Munich, and Paris, lived abroad for a long time, and returned to his home country in 1921, where he was Professor at the School of Art in Warsaw from 1925–1930. The periodical "Chimera", for which Okun produced the cover illustrated here, was named after the fire-breathing monster from the Greek myth which had the head of a lion, the body of a goat, and the tail of a serpent – a name full of symbolism for a periodical in a country which, in those years, struggled against Russia, Germany, and Austria for its national independence and achieved this from time to time only in the realm of art.

Armand Séguin (1869–1903)

29 top: Sea Landscape
Lithograph, 1893, 22.5 x 30.5 cm
29 bottom: Avenue of Trees
Etching, 1893, 18 x 30 cm
Emile Bernard (1868–1941) and Armand Séguin are the most gifted artists in the group from Pont-Aven, which we will encounter on several more occasions in this book. Séguin met van Gogh and Gauguin there too, who were an important influence on his paintings and graphic art. As a consequence of his early death, his oeuvre is not large in terms of number, but it nevertheless contains a powerful message and a high artistic value. Our illustration shows two pieces produced during his second visit to Pont-Aven in 1892/93. Both testify to Séguin's introverted nature, about which his painter friends have reported. It finds especially clear expression in the "Sea Landscape", which is wound up on the horizon, towards which three parallel lines lead, so preventing the eyes of the spectator from drifting off into the distance which is to remain shut off for him. The peaceful horizon stands in stark contrast to the waves of the landscape which is depicted in swirling lines and recalls paintings by van Gogh. In the "Avenue of Trees", Séguin's lines tangle themselves in knots even more clearly; the elliptical character of the portrayal is striking too. The tree-tops are joined together in waves, and the silhouette of the avenue resembles a wave too, rising slowly and then suddenly collapsing. The influence of Séguin on the graphic portrayal of landscapes by Edvard Munch (see 51), who had seen the work of his French colleague in Paris, is unmistakable.

Franz von Stuck (1863–1928)

57 Title page for the periodical "Jugend"
1897, length 25.6 cm
30 Title page for the periodical "Pan"
Autotype, 1895, 31.8 x 22.3 cm
The rise of Franz Stuck from being the impoverished son of a village miller to the position of "painter laureate" sounds like a modern American dream, but it took place in Munich around the turn of the century. Stuck studied there at the College of Commercial Art (1882–1884), and from 1885 at the Academy, but his professors must have seen him only very rarely: as he was completely penniless, he had to concentrate on earning his living, which he did by creating series of humoristic pictures for various magazines in Munich. Taking Böcklin, Lenbach, Holbein, and Dietz as his models, this largely self-taught artist managed to be represented at the annual exhibition in Munich in 1889. And thus began his career as a painter, graphic artist, sculptor, and architect: in 1893 he co-founded the Munich "Secession"; from 1895 he was Professor at the Academy there; at the end of the 1890s he had already earned so much money with his work that he could build the famous Stuck villa in Munich, which was his home and studio simultaneously (since 1968 it has served as a Museum of Art Nouveau, and a tourist attraction for those interested in the history of art). In 1906 he was raised to the peerage, hence the epithet "painter laureate".
His paintings represent without doubt his most impressive work, but we must ignore them in our book on the graphic arts and the art of printing created by representatives of Art Nouveau. Almost exclusively, they have erotic themes, often symbolized by dance, as in our illustration (57). One contemporary wrote: "How the senses are all blazing during a dance, how the dancers look for and find each other, how the heat of their sensations flows from their bodies and intermingles, how they surrender themselves completely, each to the other – Stuck expresses all this in a language of basic forms which is truly unique in our art". Stuck indulges here in a frenzy of line, form, and colour, the bacchanalian rhythm of the movement contributes to a decorative round-dance of lines, which, however, is restrained by the sombre background, and above all by the title of the periodical which dominates the page and seems to weigh down on the illustration. Stuck's title page for the periodical "Pan" (30), created two years earlier, seems much more moderate in style, following, as it does, models from antiquity in a manner typical of the academic school of Art Nouveau. A society formed in Berlin in 1895 named itself after the Greek god of fields, woods, shepherds, and flocks, who was the cause of sudden and inexplicable horrors; they edited, until 1900, a periodical of the same name, for bibliophiles, and with a focus on art and literature, such that the new developments in both these fields shortly before the turn of the century came together on this forum.

Edmond Aman-Jean (1860–1936)

33 Ophelia
Colour lithograph, undated, 34.3 x 26.5 cm
The French painter and graphic artist was a student of Eugène Carrière, who, together with Rodin, founded in 1890 inter alia the "Société Nationale des Beaux Arts", the second Parisian Spring Salon, and thus an association which wanted to create a middle ground between the painters of the "Académie", whose art was benumbed, and the restless avantgarde. Aman-Jean exhibited regularly in the Salon and quickly acquired a name for himself, such that he was immediately made a corresponding member from abroad when the Viennese "Secession" was founded; his work was also represented regularly at their exhibitions. In "Ver Sacrum" in 1900 his "Visions of the Splendour of Life", influenced by Edgar Degas, were praised. His subdued colours are especially characteristic, in particular the use of pink and purple, of Indian yellow and jade green. Since the 1890s Aman-Jean had been devoting himself mainly to the techniques of copperplate engraving, lithography, and watercolour painting, and he produced his numerous portraits of women, whose arabesque contours characterized the ladies of the Parisian salons very nicely, a monotonous world, a vacuum, a world of reveries, but also of sorrow, as our illustration "Ophelia" shows (the title is not certain). Aman-Jean was the first painter in France to be strongly influenced by the Pre-Raphaelites in Britain, from whose understanding of art European Art Nouveau developed.

Leon N. Bakst (1866–1924)

34 L'Après-Midi d'un Faune
Colour lithograph, 1912, cover illustration for a theatre programme.
In Leon Bakst we become acquainted with one of the most outstanding Russian representatives of Art Nouveau. Around the turn of the century two centres had formed in that country. The artists in Moscow drew their inspiration from Russian folklore (very typical for Wassily Kandinksky, see 24), determined by the rustic provinciality of their environment, and thus exerted a strong influence on the development of Western European art. Quite different were the artists in St. Petersburg, the residence of the Tsar, and centre of a rich intellectual, artistic, and social life. Looking, in keeping with tradition, to France and Germany, (there was a particularly active German and French colony with theatre and opera productions, ballet performances and concerts), the artists in St. Petersburg adopted the style of the Parisian fin-de-siècle, and constructed a dream-world of stylized forms and colours. Bakst commuted between St. Petersburg and Paris where he died. The French capital experienced from 1907 onwards a short but vehement surge in ballet. Sergej Diaghileff had founded there, with parts of the Imperial Ballet from St. Petersburg, the Russian Ballet, which achieved world fame thanks to the efforts of its members and collaborators, and which re-established classical ballet. Anna Pawlowa and Nijinsky, among others, were members of the corps de ballet; Stravinsky, among others, composed the music; and Matisse and Bakst, among others, created the costumes and stage scenery. Our illustration shows the cover illustration of the programme for the ballet "L'Après-Midi d'un Faune" by Claude Debussy; Diaghileff had entrusted the task of producing costumes and fitments to Bakst. For months Bakst observed the rehearsals, Nijinsky stood at their centre with his completely new type of choreography, which showed him marrying the veil of a nymph – a performance which caused a scandal at the premiere because of alleged immorality. The sculptor Auguste Rodin recognized, however, the sensational aspects of the portrayal: "Nijinsky possesses, to the highest degree possible, the merits of physical perfection, and harmonious and elegant proportions. In "L'Après-Midi d'un Faune", he pushes forward towards the borders of the miraculous, without any great leaps or bounds, simply by means of the comportment and movement of a creature with a semi-conscious affinity to nature. The unison of body and mime is perfect ... It is the ideal model that painters and sculptors have been trying to achieve since time immemorial". Precisely this is mirrored in Bakst's lithograph, a work of genius.

Thomas Theodor Heine (1867–1948)

35 Cover for the programme "Bühne und Brettl" ("The Stage and Cabaret")
Autotype, 1905, approx. actual size.
Like Gulbransson (see 41), T.T. Heine was a co-founder of the periodical "Simplicissimus", but he worked for other publications too, such as "Die Insel" and "Jugend". Born in Leipzig, he lived in Munich from 1889 until his emigration in 1933. His numerous book and magazine illustrations bear the mark of Japanese wood-engravings and of Beardsley's use of line, but Heine reduced the number of lines severely, thus strengthening and sharpening the message of his pictures significantly. Our illustration shows the cover for a programme of the Munich cabaret group "Die elf Scharfrichter" (The Eleven Executioners). Eleven sharp-tongued artists, including Frank Wedekind – painters, sculptors, musicians, architects and poets – came together in 1901 to attack and "execute" the society of their time in their songs and short plays. The eleven wore hangman's hoods during each performance; these are replaced in our illustration by devil's masks. "However, the actual and undisputed muse of the evenings", a contemporary reports, "was Marya Delvard. Tall and slim, in a tight black dress, she sang songs, her mouth gaping wide and fiery red". Her figure made her seem born to be the trademark of the cabaret company, and this is expressed very nicely by Heine's illustration, which was in fact employed as a poster. The doctor and author Hans Carossa saw it on display during a walk in Munich and described his impressions as follows: "A tall woman, half walking in her sleep, half as though she were a corpse, up to her chin in a black gown, stood larger than life in the foreground, two black splashes hinted at eyes, a fine curve her mouth, two dots her nose. Behind this ghostly figure, however, a choir of devil's heads, complete with horns, had emerged from the red floods, and all of them stared wide-eyed at the eerie woman, not at all diabolically, more astonished like baby fauns."

Peter Behrens (1868–1940)

36 The Kiss
Colour wood-engraving, 1898, 27.2 x 21.7 cm. Published in the periodical "Pan", Vol. 4 (1898), No. 2.
In his manifesto, "Celebrations of Life and of Art" (1900), Peter Behrens wrote: "The style of an era does not refer to the particular form of some particular art ... each type of art only shares in a style. Style, on the other hand, is the symbol of an era's overall state of health, of its whole view of life, and is mirrored in all arts as a whole". The structure of their whole life should therefore be the ultimate yardstick for assessing the art of a nation and of an era. Behrens translated this leitmotif into reality in his artistic work with a consistency rarely matched by another artist. Born in Hamburg, he co-founded the Munich "Secession" in 1893, and, four years later, the "Vereinigten Werkstätten für Kunst im Handwerk" there (already mentioned in our introduction). From 1898 onwards, he contributed to "Pan", the most important German periodical for art and literature at that time. In 1900, he was fetched to Darmstadt to work on the creation of an artist colony on the "Mathildenhöhe", an architectural complex in the Art Nouveau

style, which later became world-famous and still is today. In this way he took the step in the direction of architecture which was to be so important for the course of his life. From 1905 onwards, he received important contracts, from 1907 he was the artistic adviser of the AEG (Allgemeine Elektrizitäts-Gesellschaft; the Electricity Board), for which he constructed numerous plants, thus providing an important model for modern industrial architecture (one of his students was Walter Gropius). His private housing was designed and furnished by the artist himself, right down to the smallest detail, from the mosaic floor to the hollow tile, all in accordance with his concept of art, outlined above. Alongside such activity he created colour wood-engravings, book illustrations, posters, and printed materials, and generally busied himself in various areas of arts and crafts. His wood-engraving "The Kiss" was to epitomize German Art Nouveau. The motif mentioned in the title, showing the profiles of two faces reminiscent of Japanese prints, almost disappears amid the great waves of hair of the two; these waves do not only form a most decorative frame, they make themselves independent of the faces. The hair is a symbol of sexuality, and its surging waves hints at the rhythm of bodily union, like a whirlpool in which the lovers sink, swept away by their sexual passion.

Carl Otto Czeschka (1878–1960)
37 top: Kriemhild's Dream
Colour wood-engravings, 1908, approx. actual size.
Around the turn of the century, the publisher Gerlach & Co. represented, with its books and periodicals, including the first volume of "Ver Sacrum", an important assembly point for the graphic art of Viennese Art Nouveau. From 1897 onwards, the new series of "Allegorien" appeared there; from 1900, "Die Quelle"; and soon thereafter, the series "Gerlachs Jugendbücherei", including Volume 22, "The Nibelungen", from which the illustrations by Carl Otto Czeschka reproduced here originate. Born in Vienna, Czeschka had studied at the Academy in his home town from 1894–99, had become a member of the "Secession" in 1900, and, in 1905, a teacher at the Viennese College of Commercial Art (one of his students was Oskar Kokoschka; see 46). Finally, from 1907–1943, he was a teacher at the College of Commercial Art in Hamburg, where he also died. The incredibly versatile artist (graphics, wood-engravings, book illustrations, publications, stage scenery, interior design) – who also worked for the Vienesse Workshop, for which he designed the famous postcards – was commissioned in 1907 to paint the setting for a production of Hebbel's "Nibelungen" in the Raimund-Theater in Vienna. The production did not take place in the end, but the Nibelungen theme clearly fascinated Czeschka so much that he illustrated the Gerlach edition a year later. He was also a member of the group led by Gustav Klimt (see 47); we recognize the latter's influence in both the illustrations, which are printed side by side in our book, but which occupied a double page in the original, one opposite the other. Czeschka has produced Byzantine-like art here, rich in ornament, which we know well from Klimt's oeuvre; characteristic is the extravagant use of gold. Despite the relatively small format (our illustrations represent approximately the actual size), the pictures seem monumental, an effect determined by the large vacant black space which stands in clear contrast to the tiny, mosaic-like depictions of scenes which are reduced to what is essential; the tension between the two parts of each picture is great. Both illustrations show the beginning of the Nibelungen poem: Kriemhild wakens with a fright, for she has dreamt that two powerful eagles are killing the falcons she has reared (the ancient symbol of the loved one) – a dream which becomes tragic fact in the form of Siegfried's death. When compared to the illustration of British fairy-tales and legends, it becomes tremendously clear how much further Viennese Art Nouveau developed and what independence it attained; the judgement is permissible that we see here a peak in terms of the quality of illustration of children's books at that time, a peak which was hardly ever reached again.

Antonio Rizzi (1869–1941)
37 bottom: frontispiece for the almanac "Novissimo" 1902, 12.7 x 25.5 cm
As we will establish in our comments on Illustration 43, it is astonishing how little impact Art Nouveau made in Italy, how little the influence from elsewhere inspired an independent creative urge in artists in that country, and how varied the results were which it did unleash.
Antonio Rizzi was a Professor at the Academy in Perugia, he contributed from time to time to the periodical "Jugend", and created, besides graphic prints and illustrations, above all works in the guise of historical, genre, portrait, and scene-painter. Our illustration shows an affinity to the academic, historical Art Nouveau style, just as we know it from the works of Franz von Stuck.

Julius Diez (1870–1957)
38 Binding for the periodical "Jugend"
Raised printing on linen, 1899, 29.3 x 23.3 cm
However inviting the supposition may be, there is no evidence to suggest that the term "Jugendstil" is taken from the title of the periodical "Jugend", which appeared in Munich from 1896. This illustrated weekly with its focus on art and life, as the sub-title emphasized, did not follow a uniform "new" style, but presented alongside each other such different artists as Wilhelm Busch, Lovis Corinth, Franz von Defregger, Arnold Böcklin, Franz von Lenbach, or Franz von Stuck. By "Jugend" ("youth"), one meant more "that which is new", "that which shakes off old forms and styles", and this could also be achieved by artists who were no longer necessarily young in years. The periodical "Jugend" was open to all possible stylistic directions, united in the aim of getting beyond Naturalism and Materialism, beyond Classicism and Historicism, towards a new unconventional life-style. This goal is mirrored in the published texts which were often satirical, and critical of their times. That these tentative attempts often shot way over their goal, and later drowned in a flood of ornament, pompousness and kitsch, led to the term "Jugendstil" (first used by Rudolf Alexander Schröder in 1899, if in another context) being understood as an abusive label for a long time, until researchers established around the middle of our century what is really meant by "Jugendstil".
One of these various tentative attempts, to which "Jugend" in particular gave space, can be seen in our illustration. Whereas, for example, French Art Nouveau consciously tried to get beyond styles and forms of the 19th century, we find in Britain, and also in Art Nouveau in Munich, a clear turning towards these; this so-called second rococo represents the last repetition of historical styles in the 19th century, but these are no longer taken seriously. The use of line and lettering is semi-classical, but the inclusion of a rococo cherub is ironic.
Julius Diez studied at the College of Commercial Art and at the Academy in Munich, worked for "Jugend" from the very beginning in 1896, taught from 1907 at the College in Munich, and was a Professor at the Academy and President of the "Secession" from 1925.

Maurice Denis (1870–1943)
39 Les attitudes sont faciles et chastes
Colour lithograph, 1898, 37.9 x 27.6 cm
Like Pierre Bonnard, with whom he shared an atelier temporarily, Maurice Denis is another leading representative of the French Nabi Group which, united by the common denominator of all studying at the Académie Julian, came together in 1889 with the aim of bringing closer together the classical academic tradition and the new (Art Nouveau) style. Important for them was the composition of the figures in the picture, which was to lead to a new symbolic message by virtue of the fact that the artist managed to express their "enigmaticness". The group busied themselves intensively with the literature of the time, but also with philosophical and religious questions (hence their name from the Hebrew "nabi" = "prophets"); consequently, some of them became "nouveaux catholiques". So Denis founded the "Ateliers d'Art Sacrê" in Paris in 1919, worked almost exclusively for the Church, and eventually became a member of the Benedictine Order. The shared view of the nabi artists was that it is the task of the artist to reproduce in his picture the purity of the world, and to present the truth to the eyes of the spectator. The ideal of this way of thinking was Paradise as the state of the world before the Fall of Man (a thought which recurs in the work of Ludwig von Hofmann); the increasing industrialization and the positivistic thinking of the very end of the 19th century were seen in terms of this Fall of Man. Man was expected to find his way back to an optimistic and uncomplicated existence, freed from the laws of a questionable morality. Harmony with oneself, with one's environment, and with society, was the goal, and this need finds expression in the colour lithograph by Maurice Denis illustrated here; it comes from the cycle "Amour": the colour tones are attuned to each other, harmoniously and delicately; there are no sharp contrasts, the hair of the woman in the foreground has the same hue as the trunks and leaves of the trees; and, in terms of form too, the picture exudes calmness and harmony. This is expressed also in the title of the work, which means some thing like: "attitudes are easy and pure (chaste)".

Ferdinand Hodler (1853–1918)
40 Boy lying in a meadow of flowers
Lithograph, 1904, 96 x 64 cm. Poster of the "Secession" for the 19th Exhibition of the Austrian Association of Visual Artists.
Between 1898 and 1905 the Viennese "Secession" organized in its building 23 large art exhibitions, the 19th of which, in January and February 1904, was mainly dedicated to the Swiss painter, Ferdinand Hodler; 31 of his pictures were displayed with the result that he (at last) found recognition in Europe. At such exhibitions, the artist whose work was to be presented was usually asked to design the poster for the exhibition too; the consequence, in the case of Ferdinand Hodler, was that he produced the only graphic print he ever executed (see illustration). Typical for his Art Nouveau is the emphasis on the powerful human body, alongside which the landscape does not play a role worth mentioning. It is astonishing that Hodler never worked as a graphic artist or illustrator, for in his paintings, line, in the sketching of figures, plays an extremely important role, which had an enormously strong influence on the development of modern art.

Olaf Gulbransson (1873–1958)
41 Book-cover for "Herz ist Trumpf" (Hearts are trumps) by Korfiz Holm
Autotype, 1917, greatly enlarged.
As a counterpart to "Jugend" (see 38), there appeared in Munich from 1896 the satirical weekly "Simplicissimus", co-founded by T.T. Heine (see 35). Astonishingly, the periodical was able to be published until 1944; after the war, it was resurrected from 1954 until 1967, but did not enjoy the same resonance as in its early days. Besides political caricatures, the exuberance of life at the fin-de-siècle, above all, found expression in the illustrations, two themes, we might conclude, which are close to Art Nouveau. Among the contributors to the periodical we find all the contemporary artists who enjoyed status and fame, including Gulbransson, born in Norway, who, from 1902, worked mainly for "Simplicissimus" and helped to set the standard of the illustrations. Whether in his caricatures or in his other illustrations, he always employs the same stylistic devices: a pen-and-ink drawing portrays the action with a few short strokes; this is then confronted with a large unbroken surface, and so an effective tension between the two results. This technique is applied too in the cover illustration, reproduced here, for a novel by Korfiz Holm, who was the editor of "Simplicissimus" from 1898 until 1900, and then a worker and partner in the Munich publishing house Albert Langen, in which the periodical appeared.

Ludwig Hohlwein (1874–1949)

42 Poster for a perfumery
Lithograph, undated, greatly reduced.
The graphic artist and architect Ludwig Hohlwein studied in Munich, was an assistant at the Academy in Dresden, and went on research trips to Paris and London, until he settled in Munich where he devoted himself mainly to the art of poster-making from 1906 onwards; this art is indebted to him for important influences. He must have produced the poster, included here, for the Tochtermann perfumery in Munich at around this time. It is a picture from which fragrance seems to flow.

L.E.

43 Calendar page for the year 1900
Colour lithograph, 1899, 55 x 41.5 cm
In view of the significance which applied graphics from Italy and Italian design have nowadays, it is all the more astonishing that Art Nouveau, at least in the sphere of graphic art in printing, had almost no impact at all in the land which lies between the Adriatic and the Riviera. It is characteristic that we only know the initials of the creator (L.E.), and the date of origin (1899), when it comes to the calendar page reproduced here, which so impresses with its dynamism and wealth of colour. It was created for the Ditta Nebiolo engineering works in Turin. The few examples of Italian graphic prints in the Art Nouveau style hardly testify to a further and independent development. It rather looks as if the young generation of artists in the country omitted this phase and turned very early on to forms of Futurism and Surrealism.

Max Klinger (1857–1920)

44 Mother and Child
Etching, 1889, 19.6 x 18.3 cm
Max Klinger was one of the most important and most versatile artists in Germany at the end of the 19th and beginning of the 20th century, and greatly influenced Art Nouveau in that country. After studying in Karlsruhe and Berlin, he spent some time in Brussels and Munich, and had longer visits in Paris and Rome. In 1893 he settled in Leipzig and built a house and studio there according to his own plans. Early fame enabled him to live as a freelance graphic artist, painter, and sculptor. From 1884 onwards, he produced numerous murals and friezes for private villas; from 1899 he devoted himself mainly to sculpture. At that time he also produced his most famous work, the Beethoven Monument for the Museum of Fine Arts in Leipzig; he added an extension to the museum in order to be able to erect and illuminate this work properly. In the early years of his period of productivity, however, we find cycles of graphic work (etchings, engravings, lithographs). Our illustration is taken from the cycle "On Death", in which it was the eleventh item. The combination of various styles, such as Classicism, Romanticism and Art Nouveau, in Klinger's work is irritating; none of these individual styles is worked in so fully that it dominates. They are masterly in terms of technical execution, but Klinger's pictures swing to and fro between the purely decorative (like the frame in our illustration) and enigmatic symbols which can hardly be decoded, since they are often executed in a naturalistic style which appears even to offset the symbolism. The world portrayed seems like a fantastic construction, and can also be seen as precursor of Surrealism.

Gustave Henri Jossot (born 1866)

45 Abendlohe
Autotype, 1897, 20 x 18.2 cm. Published in the periodical "Jugend".
The French painter and graphic artist worked mainly as an illustrator for newspapers and magazines in Paris, but also, as our illustration shows, for "Jugend", which was published in Munich. In the years between 1895 and 1911 his paintings were presented at numerous exhibitions in Paris. Around 1920, he converted to Islam and began to call himself Abdul Karim Jossot; we lose trace

of his life at this point, such that we do not know when he died. Typical of his graphic prints are their two-dimensional character, and the minimal use of contrasting colours, which he did not develop. In our illustration, for example, the dark silhouettes of the trees stand out against the burning red of the evening sun; green is used to suggest the moist coolness of the forest floor.

Oskar Kokoschka (1886–1980)

46 Sleeping Woman
Colour lithograph, 1908, 29 x 24 cm
In the case of Oskar Kokoschka, one of the most famous painters of the Modern Era, we wish to comment, in the context of our book, on only his early period as a painter and illustrator, which reveals links with Art Nouveau. From 1904 onwards, he studied at the College of Commercial Art in Vienna, and was strongly influenced by Klimt (see 47). A fellow student was Lilith, in whom he fell madly in love, but his love remained unrequited. Kokoschka portrays this encounter and its whirl of emotions in his book, "The Dreaming Boys", 500 copies of which were printed by the publishing house of the Viennese Workshop in 1908; it attracted hardly any attention and became a failure (nowadays it is auctioned for high prices). Our illustration shows the motif on the title page. The dreaming girl (Lilith) is surrounded by the waters of a moat, in which predatory red fish await their catch. The symbolism is clear: the lines of the water as the web of fate which is spun around the girl, in which she is caught, and which can lead to tragic entanglements, as already indicated by the fish representing the compulsive danger of eros. In his autobiography, "My Life", Kokoschka wrote of this book: "The original assignment was to draw a children's book . . . it was to contain colour lithographs. But I stuck to the task only on the first page (our illustration). The other pictures were then created, together with my verses, to form freely-composed poetry in pictures. I call the book that because it was a kind of report, in words and pictures, on my emotional state at that time". The text which Kokoschka composed to accompany the pictures typifies in its expressiveness the raging feelings in the young artist. But his illustrations also anticipate Expressionism; he later became the leading representative of that style.

Gustav Klimt (1862–1918)

47 Theseus and the Minotaur, cover illustration for "Ver Sacrum"
Autotype, 1898 (Double Number 5/6), 29.1 x 28.4 cm (Cover of that issue).
No artist made a greater overall contribution to Art Nouveau in Vienna than Gustav Klimt. After studying at the Viennese College of Commercial Art (1876–1883), he formed a team, together with his brother and another painter, which produced numerous joint pieces of work until 1892, mainly murals and ceiling frescos for theatres in the style of historicism. In 1892 his brother died, and Klimt went through a crisis, unleashed by artistic and stylistic questions. True, his works had already found much recognition by then, but he felt that through their historicism they were still too attached to the old Viennese School. This school had organized itself in the form of an association of artists, to which Klimt and numerous other young artists belonged too. A dispute between the older and the younger generation led in 1897 to the resignation of a group of young artists from the association. A Klimt Group was formed, and from it grew, that same year, the Viennese "Secession"; Klimt was a founding member and its first President (until 1899). At that same time, Klimt's artistic crisis also ended, and an incredibly productive phase began, which includes many paintings and about 400 drawings. They almost all revolve around erotic themes and portray the transitoriness of physical love – the moment of greatest ecstasy and bliss, which seems to last an eternity, but the end of which, in reality, is in sight, and leads to sadness, a favourite theme of Art Nouveau. Conservative circles in the Viennese bourgeoisie condemned Klimt as a pornographer, his works gave rise to scandals, and yet he became at that time the leading

painter in Austria. In 1905, he broke away from the "Secession": the Klimt Group resigned to a man. Thereafter Klimt looked more towards Germany (Berlin, Munich), but he retained his studio in Vienna. His most famous students were Egon Schiele and Oskar Kokoschka (see 46); he would have been appointed Professor at the Viennese Academy of Art but for an objection by the Austrian archduke Franz Ferdinand. Our illustration shows an example of his printed graphics. Klimt had designed the motif "Theseus and the Minotaur" in 1898 for the poster to publicize the first exhibition by the "Secession". The poster aroused displeasure at the Viennese Board of Censors, and so our illustration shows the censored version, which was used as a cover for "Ver Sacrum", the organ of the «Secession": the sexual part of Theseus is now hidden by a tree-trunk. More important than the depiction of the battle between Theseus and the Minotaur, taken from the Greek myth and presented here in a frieze (in the style of historicism), is the figure of Pallas Athene on the right side of the picture. The Viennese "Secession" adopted her as their "patron goddess", and she features in many posters of this association. Her shield displays a Gorgon's head, the head of one of the snake-haired sisters in the Greek myth, whose looks turned to stone anyone who saw them. Significant, too, is the large, vacant, almost square surface in the motif, which is possibly intended to symbolize the distance between the male and female principles.

Walter Leistikow (1865–1908)

48 top: Flying Cranes
Colour lithograph, 1899, 21.5 x 27.6 cm
In 1883, after only a few months of his course at the Academy in Berlin, Walter Leistikow was dismissed because of lack of talent. He continued his studies with the help of private tutors until 1887, then devoted himself to the design of carpets, wallpaper, and furniture, decorative pieces of work, in which Scandinavian motifs combined with elements of Art Nouveau. In the mid 1890s he discovered those motifs which were to make him famous: monumental and decorative depictions of the landscape around Berlin. His expulsion from the Academy had scarred his personality, despite all his later success, and made him join a group of young artists who revolted against the established thoughts on art which prevailed in the capital of Imperial Germany. In 1898 he therefore co-founded the Berlin "Secession", and in 1904 was involved in the founding of the German Artists' Association. His graphic works appeared mostly in the periodical "Pan" (see 30), so, too, the lithograph reproduced here from the year 1899. Leistikow used the motif of cranes and swans, so too in wallpaper and carpets. The appeal of the illustration lies in its stylized decorative aspect: the clouds are represented by brick-red strips, a yellowish green surface forms the sky, and the birds hang low and heavy in the air, seeming almost to be an anti-symbol of flight. They move from right to left, whereas the spectator's gaze normally shifts in the exact opposite direction.

Emil Orlik (1870–1932)

48 bottom: Fuji pilgrims
Colour wood-engraving, 1900, 23.9 x 42 cm
Emil Orlik, born in Prague, was one of the few European artists who studied the Japanese wood-engraving, of such decisive influence on Art Nouveau, in the country of its origin. After studying in Munich, he went on numerous trips to Holland, Paris, England, and, in 1900/1901, Japan. From 1903 he lived in Vienna where he became a member of the "Secession", from which, however, he resigned in 1905, together with the Klimt Group. That same year, he was appointed Professor at the Museum of Applied Arts in Berlin, which remained his new home town until his death. There he met Max Reinhardt who, in the first quarter of the 20th century, above all by means of his new treatment of stage technique, achieved a completely new form of theatre; for Reinhardt's productions, Orlik designed the costumes and set.

In Europe, and especially Germany, around the turn of the century, Japan was truly in fashion; the little civilized and largely still untouched Far East held a great attraction, presumably as a consequence of people being weary of life in Europe with its widespread emphasis on technology and commerce. Information on this far-off world was derived above all from the novels of the English author Lafcadio Hearn, who lived in Japan from 1890 until his death in 1904. Orlik illustrated a number of the German translations of these books. The fairy-tale qualities of the Eastern world, emphasized by the use of gold, combine here with decorative elements, such as we know them from Viennese Art Nouveau. This wood-engraving, which might almost be confused with a Japanese original, was produced during Orlik's travels to Japan; the accentuated and stylized presentation of the pilgrims contrasts with the scissor-cut-like depiction of the trees in the background.

Max Kurzweil (1867–1916)
49 The Cushion
Colour wood-engraving, 1903, 28.5 x 26 cm
Even in his lifetime Max Kurzweil was little-known, although he was a founding member of the Viennese "Secession", which he left in 1905, together with the Klimt Group, and although he created numerous illustrations for "Ver Sacrum". Prior to that, he had studied at the Viennese Academy and, for a short time, at the Académie Julian in Paris. Conscripted during World War I, he became a war painter in 1916 and committed suicide that same year, presumably as a result of his desperation at his separation from his wife, who was surprised by the beginning of the war when back home in France, the country she was not then permitted to leave again. Many of his paintings and wood-engravings show his wife, as does our illustration, which appeared in 1903 in the annual portfolio of the Viennese Society for Reproductive Arts; Kurzweil's picture raised a great stir, then as now (a few years ago a very popular re-print was issued). This wood-engraving, in which five colours are employed, is his best-known work, and was often interpreted psychologically. The woman's bearing, as well as the lines in the patterns of the sofa and the cushion, direct the spectator's attention to the woman's hand; her thumb is in the shade, her index finger well apart from her other three. The number three symbolizes the male principle, from which the female is separated in the form of the index finger – possibly pointing to a resolve to achieve emancipation. This is likewise suggested by the fact that the woman's body is swathed in cloth, and her face is hidden – a sign of her refusal of man?

Alfons Maria Mucha (1860–1939)
50 Poster for JOB
Colour lithograph, 1899, 53 x 40 cm
The invention of the advertising pillar in 1855 made it necessary to think anew about the role of the poster as an advertising device; designers had to adapt to the taste of the wide public, in an attempt to win its attention. This new art of poster-making was created in the 1890s by Toulouse-Lautrec (see 60), who was responsible for its highlights at that time, but the contribution of Mucha, born in Bohemia, was decisive too. Mucha lived in Vienna from 1877, where he worked as a scene-painter. He then studied in Munich, and from 1887 onwards at private academies in Paris. In 1894 he created his first poster for the famous French actress, Sarah Bernhardt, whose art he was to accompany from then on with his posters. In this way he had discovered Art Nouveau; in Paris people even spoke about the "Mucha Style". Shortly before World War I, he returned to Prague, where he produced a series of monumental pictures, making him the most important artist of those years in his home country. Our illustration shows a poster for the firm JOB, a producer of cigarette papers. It was printed in four colours and gold, a masterpiece in terms of technique, hardly matched by our modern processes of reproduction. We can only guess, for example, at the gold tones in the lady's hair. Mucha obviously knew much, but probably subconsciously, about the psychology of advertising: the cigarette paper, for which customers are to be won, does not play any role in the poster; even the firm's name disappears in the background. The female figure has moved into the foreground, her facial expression, suggestive of a connoisseur, stands in strong contrast, full of tension, to the swirling waves of her hair, a symbol of eroticism. What man could resist the powerful message of such a poster, which promised not only the enjoyment of the perfect cigarette, but also erotic adventure?

Edvard Munch (1863–1944)
51 Madonna – Loving Woman – Conception
Colour lithograph, 1895/1902, 60.5 x 44.2 cm
The Norwegian Munch, known to us today more as the co-founder and leading representative of Expressionism, contributed to Art Nouveau too. He led a restless life in every respect. He studied in Oslo and Paris, numerous study trips took him again and again to Germany, Italy, and France, where he spent a lengthy period of time, before returning to Norway for good in 1909. His third stay in Paris from 1895 onwards led to an important turning-point for his artistic development; there he became acquainted with the most significant representatives of the New Style in France, e.g. Gauguin, van Gogh, Toulouse-Lautrec, Bernard, Denis, and Séguin (with the single exception of van Gogh, these men are all represented in this volume). From these artists Munch adopted stylistic devices, but not without having reappraised them intellectually. In his case, a creative shaping of human experience was also included, and in such a way that the spectator can relate directly to his works, however subjectively they may be portrayed. The central experience which has an effect throughout Munch's life, and which is reflected in all his works, is the experience of fear, lack of personal contact, and solitude. As a young man he had a traumatic experience with a woman, and this led to mixed feelings towards the opposite sex: he was as fascinated by the female's surrender to the male at the moment of coitus, and by the relinquishing of the self involved in that, as he was afraid of the moment which follows, when heavenly love is abruptly exchanged again for reality and its banality, with the battle of the sexes, such as it found literary expression in the dramas of Munch's contemporaries, Ibsen and Strindberg. Munch's emotional problems led to a nervous breakdown, from which he recovered in 1908/1909 in a nursing home. This moment marks exactly a break in his artistic creation. The phase of Art Nouveau has ended, further development in the direction of Expressionism has taken place. The colour lithograph illustrated here (Indian ink and chalk on stone; the self-coloured stone originates from the year 1895, the coloured stones from 1902) is very much typical of Munch's artistic translation of the crisis in his life. We see a woman, surrendering at the moment of coitus, from the perspective of the man bending over her. The depiction of her face and body suggests Madonna-like qualities, they are surrounded by blue and black wavy lines, symbolizing love and passion. Decorative elements, painted on the frame of the picture, and readily identifiable as spermatozoons, enlarged as though under a microscope, head towards her vagina, and thus allude to the moment of conception. They come from a figure in the bottom left hand corner of the picture and return indirectly to it – thus symbolizing conception and birth, but also the man (and thus Munch) who feels just as helpless vis-à-vis a woman as an embryo.

Emil Nolde (1867–1956)
52 Storm
Hand-painted wood-engraving, 1906, 15.5 x 19 cm
In this volume we have already been able to observe on several occasions the transition from Art Nouveau to Expressionism, e.g. in the work of Kokoschka (see 46) and Munch (51). It is reflected, too, in the wood-engraving included here by Emil Nolde. The artist was originally called Hansen; as a pseudonym he used the name of his birthplace, Nolde on Jutland. From 1885–1889 he did an apprenticeship as a wood carver; he then taught at the trade school in Saint Gallen/Switzerland from 1892–1898; from 1899 onwards, he turned to painting (training in Munich, Paris, and Copenhagen). In 1905 he moved to Dresden, and, until 1907, was a member of the group of expressionist artists there known as "Die Brücke" (The Bridge). They created their own style which, without freeing itself from the representational altogether, sought to heighten expression by means of crudely simplified forms, and strong, often garish, colours. This is shown clearly by our illustration. In 1906, Nolde had published a portfolio of ten wood-engravings, to which our picture "Storm" also belongs; these fairy-tale illustrations were printed in black and white. Individual pictures in this series were coloured by hand by Nolde; these rarities are now much sought-after by art dealers.
After a trip around the world in 1913/14, Nolde alternated between his home in Berlin and his farm in Seebüll/Sleswick-Holstein.
After 1933 the National Socialists declared Nolde's art to be "entartet" (degenerate); they confiscated 1,052 works from museums, and banned him from painting.

Lucien Pissarro (1863–1944)
53 Illustration for "Aucassin and Nicolette"
Colour wood engraving, 1897, 12.2 x 11.9 cm
The French painter and graphic artist Lucien Pissarro, the oldest son of the famous representative of Impressionism and Pointillism, Camille Pissarro, under whom he also studied painting, emigrated to Great Britain after his studies, where he collaborated with Charles Rickett at the latter's Vale Press. In 1894 he founded, together with his wife, the Eragny Press, which published 32 books by 1914. From 1900 onwards, the printing press was situated in London-Hammersmith, also the home of the Kelmscott Press of the most important British typographer and creator of artistic books, William Morris. Our example shows an illustration for "Aucassin and Nicolette", the famous Old-French novella (around 1200), a love story, which was published in 1897 by Macmillan of London, but printed by Pissaro at his Eragny Press. The decorative frame is in keeping with the thoughts on artistic books of a William Morris or Walter Crane (see 21), but unlike these two, Pissarro simplified the ornamental motifs. In their clarity they harmonize very nicely with the typeface and the wood-engraving illustration.

Joseph Sattler (1867–1931)
54 Illustration for the Nibelungen poem
1898–1904, our illustration is about half the size of the original.
Illustrating the Nibelungen poem was a favourite task of German and Austrian representatives of Art Nouveau. Examples of this can be found in the present book in the work of Braune (see 17) and Czeschka (37). Viewed as an artist, Joseph Sattler stands between these two. Trained in Munich, he was employed to teach at the College of Commercial Art in Strasburg, worked from 1895 until 1904 in Berlin, then returned to Strasburg, before finally settling down in Munich in 1918. The illustrations for the Nibelungen were created during his time in Berlin (our example shows how Hagen sinks the Nibelung hoard in the Rhine), and were printed on pergament by the Reichsdruckerei in Berlin in 1900 to mark the Great Exhibition in Paris. In terms of their two-dimensionality and their closeness to Historicism, they differ tellingly from the over-ornamental cover illustrations created by Sattler from 1895 onwards for the periodical "Pan" (see 30).

Iwan J. Bilibin (1876–1942)
55 Red Rider (Midday or the Sun)
1902, 22.2 x 14.7 cm. Illustration for the fairy-tale "Wassilissa the Beautiful".
Like Bakst (see 34), Bilibin comes from the circle of artists in St. Petersburg, where he was born and studied from 1895–98. Following sojourns in Italy and Switzerland, he left Russia in 1918 and lived in France until 1936; then

he returned to the Soviet Union. Besides working as a set-designer, Bilibin devoted himself mainly to the illustration of Russian folktales and heroic poetry; he achieved his highlights around the turn of the century. His ornamental and decorative style places him firmly in the group of the few Russian representatives of Art Nouveau; his rich and imaginative use of colours (here, the red horse, which symbolizes mid-day and the sun) corresponds to the narrative wealth of Russian folktales.

Carl Strathmann (1866–1939)
56   Cover for the songbook "Totentanz" (Danse macabre)
Colour lithograph, undated, approx. actual size.
Born in Düsseldorf, Strathmann studied at the Academy there from 1882–1886; he was eventually dismissed for being untalented. From 1886–1889 he continued his studies at the School of Art in Weimar, and then moved to Munich, where he remained for the rest of his life, and where he achieved his artistic breakthrough. With his caricatures for the periodicals "Jugend" and "Fliegende Blätter" he attained great popularity, whereas his paintings and lithographs were more disputed. Typically, they are inundated with ornament, as our illustration shows. They are composed of many carefully drawn patterns, covering the surface of the picture like a carpet, and filling every last corner, in a manner reminiscent of Byzantine mosaics – a stylistic device found in the work of Franz von Stuck (see 57).

Jan Toorop (1858–1928)
58   Swan Maidens
Colour lithograph, 1892, 23.1 x 19.9 cm
The artistic oeuvre of the Dutch painter, graphic artist, and handicrafter Jan Toorop was labelled by contemporaries a synopsis of the history of art in the last four decades of the nineteenth century, so many influences can be perceived, so many made an impact on his work. In our illustration we see reflected the art of drawing commanded by Beardsley (see 14, 15); but also the lightness of touch of Jessie King (25); and the force of Peter Behrens (36). The representational depiction of the girl in the flowing garment is contrasted by the undulating lines which make the dress, the water, and her hair seem arabesque. The girl is approached by two swans; this ancient motif from Greek mythology, in which Leda becomes the lover of Zeus, the greatest of the Greek gods, who takes the form of a swan to approach her, has often been employed in art. The mysteriousness of this dream-like scene demands an interpretation, but Toorop was not interested in that; only the enigmatic atmosphere mattered to him, which he achieved by the purely decorative and ornamental aspects of the composition. In this manner, Art Nouveau reaches a dead end which permits of no further modification; we were previously able to observe a similar development in the work of Fritz Endell (see 23).

Henri de Toulouse-Lautrec (1864–1901)
59   Poster for Aristide Bruant
Lithograph, 1893, 65.6 x 48 cm
Henri de Toulouse-Lautrec was surely the most bizarre apparition on the Parisian art scene around the turn of the century, but he nevertheless must be regarded as one of those artists who have given a major impulse to Modern Art. Of noble birth, a member of one of the oldest families in the country, he should have been assured a life of luxury, but things were to turn out differently. At the age of 14 he broke one leg, at 15 the other, symptoms of a serious bone disease which was to cripple him. His head and body developed normally, his legs remained short. During his long illness he began to draw, then he studied painting at private academies from 1880 to 1887, and became acquainted there with Bernard and van Gogh among others. The paintings he produced at this time were still very closely attached to Impressionism. He painted exactly what he saw. Toulouse-Lautrec liked to frequent the artistic cabarets of Montmartre, he even set up his studio there – another

decision which was to affect the rest of his life. For in 1890 the giant dance hall "Moulin Rouge" was opened, and Toulouse-Lautrec was commissioned to design a publicity poster for it. Although he had never worked as a poster artist, he accepted the assignment, and created his masterpiece which was soon to be displayed on every wall in the area. The world of cafés, cabarets, and prostitutes, the circus and the race course, were now the new home of this cripple who was thirsty for life, who wanted to see and experience everything. We know this world from hundreds of lithographs which he produced. He heightened the sensual passion of his observations still more by consuming alcohol in immoderate quantities; the fact that he overexploited his body in this way, and his awareness that as a cripple he was, in the final analysis, still an outsider, led to a nervous breakdown in 1897; two years later, his mother took it into her hands to have him committed to a psychiatric hospital, an action which hurt the artist very deep down; in 1901 his vitality was finally and permanently exhausted.
With his poster for the "Moulin Rouge" he had found his way to a new style, to his style, familiar to us from more than 30 other posters, which have influenced the use of graphics in advertising in the whole of Europe. What was new in these was his scant but powerful use of line; the inclusion of generous unbroken surfaces, reminiscent of Japanese wood-engravings; and coloration which was rich in contrast – three criteria which were brought to masterly perfection in the poster for Aristide Bruant (reproduced here without the accompanying text). Toulouse-Lautrec's depiction led to the silhouette of the popular music-hall singer becoming an unmistakable trademark – which sums up the goal of modern advertising.

Heinrich Vogeler (1872–1942)
60   Cover picture and title page for "Der Kaiser und die Hexe" (The Emperor and the Witch)
Autotype, 1900, 20.2 x 25.3 cm
This piece of work is without doubt a highlight in the production of artistic books by German representatives of the Art Nouveau; Heinrich Vogeler is an outstanding example of this group. Three people or institutions contributed to this highlight at the beginning of a path which was to lead to great fame: Vogeler; Hugo von Hofmannsthal, the author of the drama "Der Kaiser und die Hexe", which, with its spirit of melancholy and scepticism, was in keeping with the atmosphere of fin-de-siècle; and the Insel publishing company, founded in 1899, which printed 200 copies of this magnificent work on pergament, and from which the leading German publisher of literary and artistic books in the first half of the 20th century was to develop. A volume of poetry by Vogeler was the first book published by the company; Hofmannsthal remained its most important author for decades. Vogeler lived from 1895 onwards on a farm in the village of Worpswede near Bremen, which had become an artists' colony in 1889 and still is today. In the aftermath of World War I, Vogeler turned to Socialism and Communism and lived from 1932 in the Soviet Union where he also died; as a painter he switched to socialist realism.

Friedrich König (1857–1941)
61   Market stalls at the Viennese Naschmarkt
Wood-engraving, 1903, 15 x 14 cm
Friedrich König was also a founding member of the Viennese "Secession". After studying in Vienna and Munich, he returned to his home town and was active there as a wood engraver; he worked above all on the volume "The Austrian Monarchy in Words and Pictures". Book illustration was his main field of work, and thus he became one of the most important illustrators of the periodical "Ver Sacrum", for which he produced a delightful series of scenes from the Viennese Naschmarkt in 1903, including the example reproduced here. The Naschmarkt was at that time the central food market in the Austrian capital (its name has nothing to do with the German verb "naschen" [= to nibble], even

if it is tempting to think so). The fine lady shopped there just as much as the servant girl. The appeal of the rows of stalls with their colourful supply of foods from all over the world, coupled with the proverbial quick-wittedness of the market-women, is very nicely expressed in this atmospheric scene.

Koloman Moser (1868–1918)
62   Woglinde
Pen and ink, 1901, 17.1 x 19 cm. Illustration for the month of July in the "Ver Sacrum" calendar of 1901.
His inventive imagination and versatility meant that Koloman Moser was one of the most important artists in Austria around 1900. From about 1897 onwards, his artistic activity was devoted almost exclusively to commercial art; he produced posters, book ornamentation, glass windows, designs for furniture, postcards, postage stamps, bank notes etc. In 1886 he had started studying at the Viennese Academy of Visual Arts, and had added to this another period of study from 1892–95 at the Viennese College of Commercial Art, where he met Gustav Klimt (see 47). He was a founding member of the "Secession", which he left in 1905 with the Klimt Group. In 1903 he co-founded the Viennese Workshop and remained a member until 1907. Besides illustrations in children's books, his graphic works appeared mainly in "Ver Sacrum"; he was (alongside Klimt) the most important collaborator on this periodical, in which the illustrations included here were printed as the pages of a calendar.
Illustration 62 shows a (fictitious) scene from the Nibelungen legend: the Rhine Maiden Woglinde examines a precious stone from the Nibelungen hoard. Interesting comparisons can be made with Czeschka (see 37) and Sattler (54), who have illustrated the same legend. In Moser's work, two-dimensionality plays a major role, as does the contrast between black and white. The generous unbroken surfaces lend the whole a powerful dynamism. The spectator is tempted to turn the picture round by ninety degrees, such that the bearing of the girl seems more natural (and we see that to which our eyes are accustomed), but that is the telling twist in this pen-and-ink drawing: Moser has the Rhine Maiden move just like the fish which swarm around her, in gold, as if they had already swallowed the Nibelungen hoard. For Moser it is also typical that he works the word "July" into the decoration on the frame, thus achieving a unity of text and decorative elements.

Albert Weisgerber (1878–1915)
63   Peacock Dance
Gouache, 1902, 33.6 x 27.9 cm (Kohl-Weigand Collection, St. Ingbert).
Weisgerber, a skilled interior decorator, studied at the Academy in Munich shortly before the turn of the century, and later became a student of Stuck (see 30, 57).- Between 1897 and 1912 he was incredibly productive as an illustrator, creating approximately 500 pieces of work for the periodical "Jugend" alone. The illustration reproduced here was intended for that publication too, but did not get beyond the design stage. In terms of age, Weisgerber did not belong to the actual generation of most Art Nouveau representatives, but his early works were strongly influenced by them. He was killed in the First World War.

Ludwig von Zumbusch (1861–1927)
64   Title page for the periodical "Jugend"
1897, 27 x 20.7 cm
Alphabetical order would have it that our book closes with two illustrations for the periodical "Jugend", which have a similar theme, but which were executed in entirely different ways.
Weisgerber's gouache (63), despite the joyful dance portrayed, seems relatively scrupulous and laden with symbolism, whereas in Zumbusch's pair of dancing girls the sheer joie de vivre of a young generation finds expression, of the very generation which gave the periodical its title. Zumbusch studied at the academies in Vienna, Munich, and Paris, and was a member of the Munich "Secession".

FEBRUAR

The Chap-Book

Being A MISCELLANY of Curious and Interesting Songs, Ballads, Tales, Histories, &c.; adorned with a variety of pictures and very delightful to read: *newly composed* by MANY CELEBRATED WRITERS: To which are annex'd a LARGE COLLECTION of Notices of BOOKS

WILL H BRADLEY 1895

Hugo L. Braune

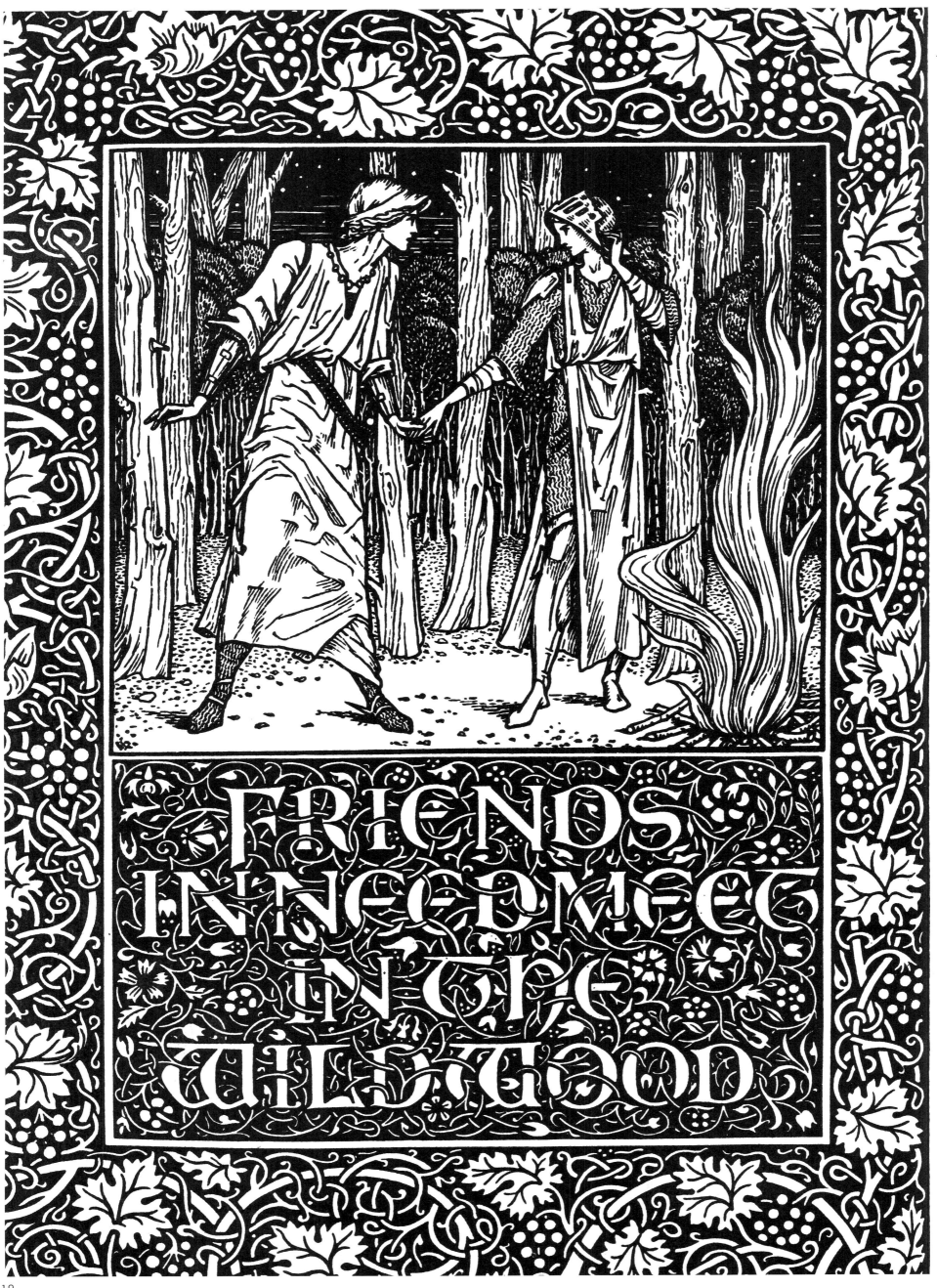

FRIENDS IN NEED MEET IN THE WILD WOOD

While
PRETTY MAIDS
all of them pass

With careless hearts quite un-heeding.

DIE ARCHITEKTONISCHEN SKIZZEN DIESES HEFTES.

Dem Tempo des modernen Lebens entspricht es, dass uns Variationen eines einmal gefundenen künstlerischen Gedankens nicht mehr befriedigen, dass wir vielmehr einen wahren Heisshunger und eine unglaubliche Verdauungsfähigkeit in Bezug auf neue Ideen entwickeln. Die aus früheren Kunstperioden stammenden oder solchen anhängenden Architekten traten neuen Aufgaben, wenigstens in Bezug auf die Formensprache, zunächst mit compilatorischen Absichten gegenüber; die modern empfindenden dagegen trachten einem neuen Problem zunächst mit ihrem künstlerischen Empfinden nahe zu kommen und aus dieser primären baulichen Empfindung wächst dann die Erfindung der angemessenen Form heraus. Lange schon sind wir gewöhnt, die Skizzen der Maler und Bildhauer mit ernstem Interesse zu betrachten. Warum sollen wir dasselbe nicht auch den flüchtigen Niederschreibungen allererster, allerpersönlichster Gedanken der Baukünstler entgegenbringen? Als solche Notierungen allererster baulicher Gedanken aber wollen die architektonischen Skizzen dieses Heftes betrachtet werden. Der Weg von ihnen bis zum fertigen Bauplane ist ein weiter, aber nicht weiter als der von der Skizze des Malers, des Bildhauers, zum fertigen Gemälde, zur Statue. V. S.

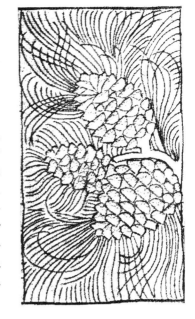

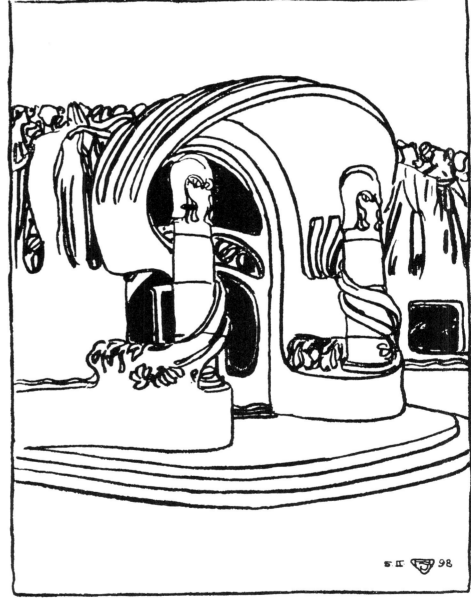

The Colour Plates

"L'APRES MIDI D'UN FAUNE
(NIJINSKY)

4me Année   No 16
15 Mai 1912
Numéro Exceptionnel
60 Pages

PRIX
1 fr. 50

7me Saison
des
BAKST
Ballets
Russes

Bühne und Brettl

III. Jahrg.
No. 4.

Preis
20 Pfg.

Elf Scharfrichter-Nummer

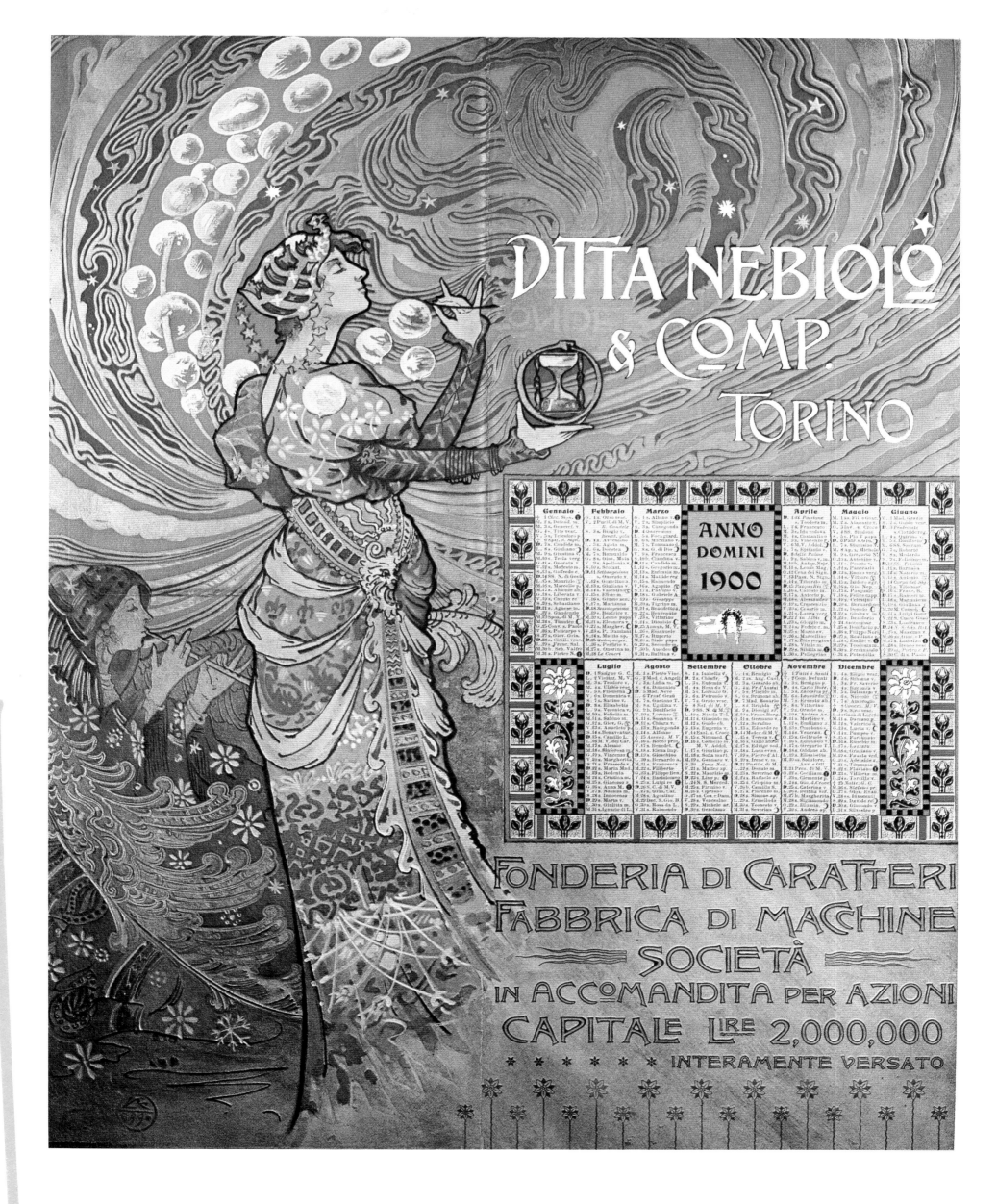

44

"ET DE LE FOILLE AUTRESI,
UNE BELLE LOGE EN FIST."

DER KAISER UND DIE HEXE

VON HUGO VON HOFMANNSTHAL
MIT ZEICHNUNGEN VON HEINRICH
VOGELER-WORPSWEDE
ERSCHIENEN IM VERLAGE DER
INSEL BEI SCHUSTER & LÖFFLER
BERLIN S.W. IM MAI 1900